This book belongs to:

Copyright 2024 ©

Positive Dungeons

How to Use This Book

Disconnect from the Outside World
Switch off your phone or put it on airplane mode to enjoy a
moment of tranquility and focused immersion.

Prepare Your Space
Choose a comfortable, well-lit space. Consider some soft background
music and a relaxing drink to accompany your coloring session.

There Are No Rules in Art
There are no wrong choices in art.
Feel free to experiment with your color palette.

Explore and Experiment
This book is ideally suited for colored pencils or markers.
Please use wet mediums with caution.
To safeguard against any potential bleed-through from markers,
consider placing a cardstock sheet behind the page you're coloring.

Practice Mindfulness
Let each stroke guide you toward a meditative state. Concentrate
on your hand's movement and how the color fills each space.

Personalize Your Experience
Feel free to add your own details to the illustrations to
further personalize your artwork.

**Remember, each page of this book is an invitation to explore mythical
worlds and rediscover the joy of creating. Happy Coloring!**

Share Your Thoughts!
Enjoy Our Summer Coloring Book

Get ready to feel the summer vibes and dive into a world of joy with our delightful Summer Coloring Book! Let your imagination soar as you infuse these pages with vibrant hues, bringing sunny scenes to life. Our aim is to spark joy and ignite your creativity, and we can't wait to see the magnificent artworks you'll create!

GET READY FOR HOURS OF COLORING FUN!

If our coloring book brings smiles to your Life, we'd be grateful for your kind words in a review. Follow the instructions at the end of the book to share your feedback. Your reviews help us continue creating joy-filled experiences for young artists like yours!

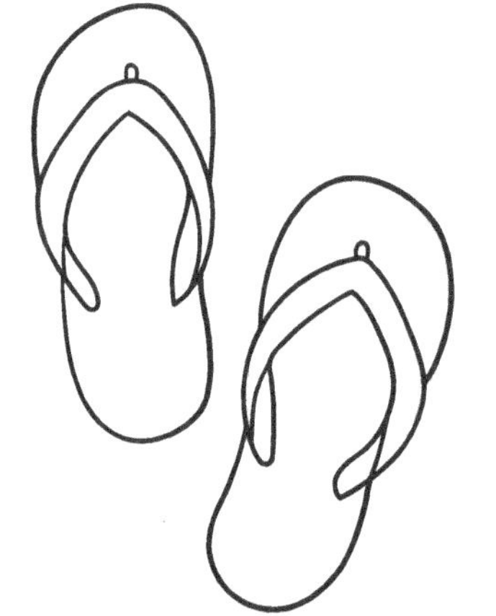

COLOR TEST

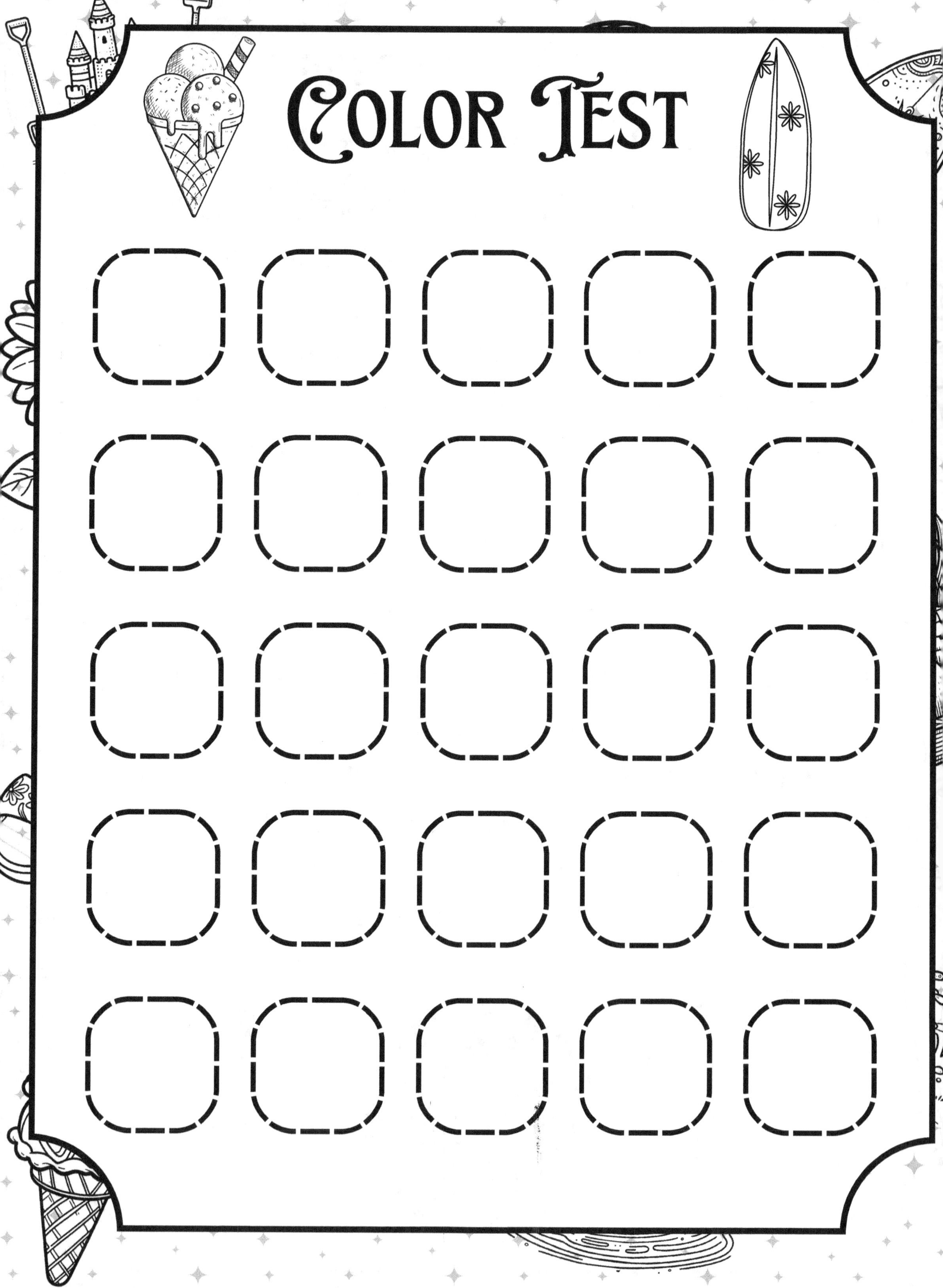

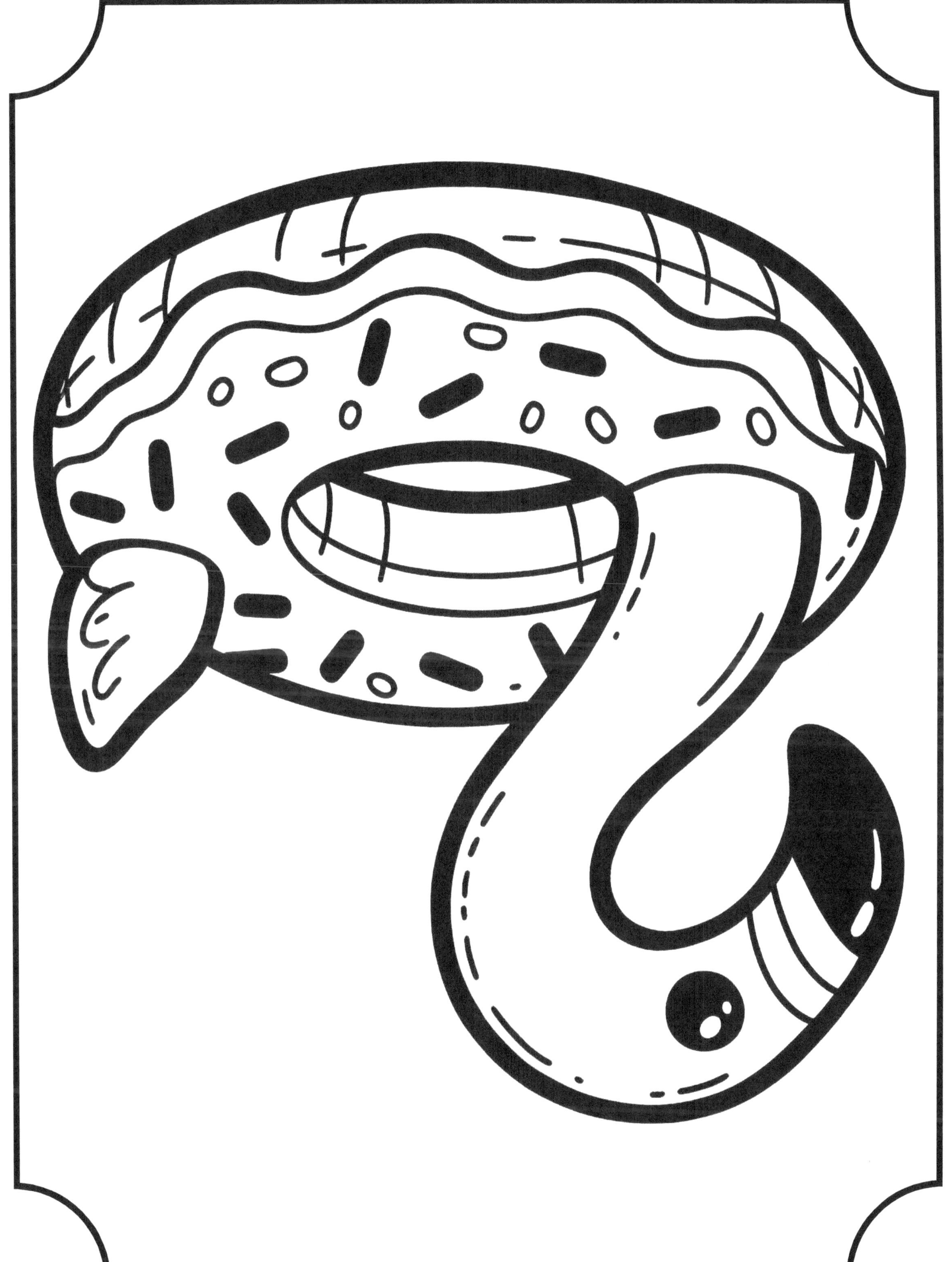

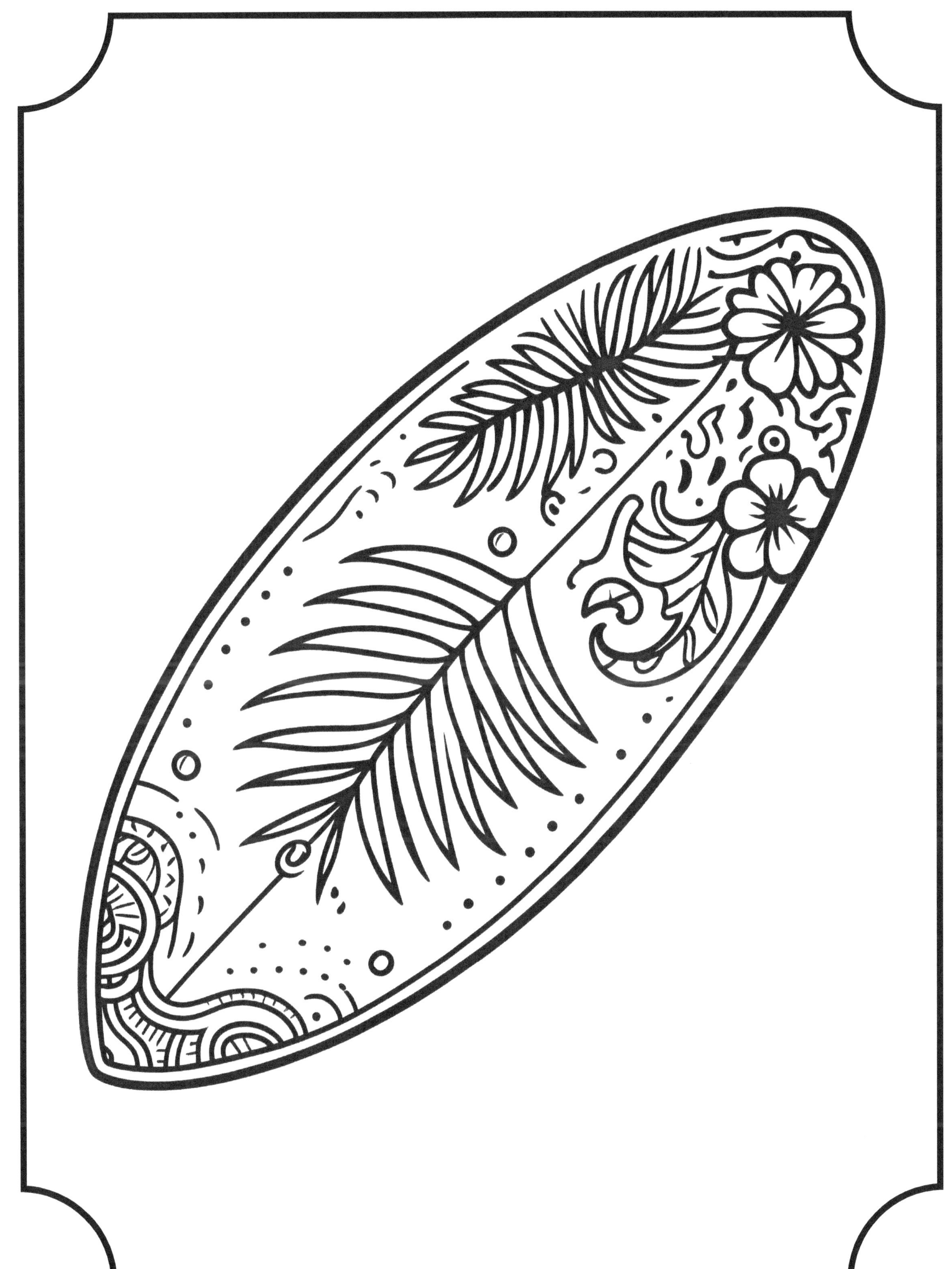

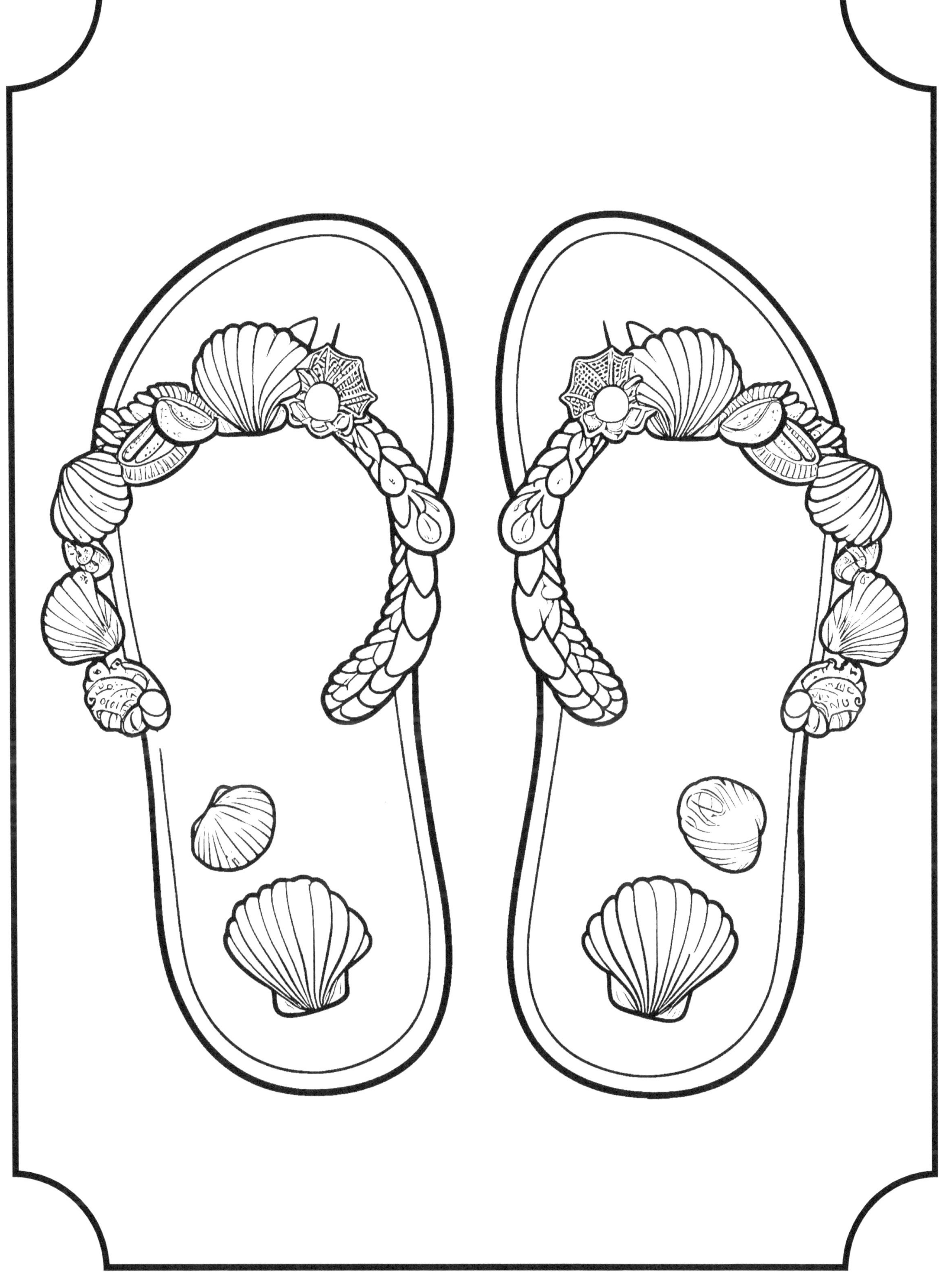

DID YOU ENJOY OUR BOOK?

Looking for a greater challenge?

If you enjoy our book, we'd love to hear from you! If you want, you can share your thoughts in a review and tell us what kind of activity book you'd like next.

Follow us on social media to stay updated on when we release more special books just for you!

Search for us as **Positive Dungeons**.

We want to express our sincerest gratitude for dedicating your time to enjoy our book. We understand that time is a precious resource, and we greatly appreciate the fact that you have chosen to spend some of yours with us.

We would love to hear your thoughts about our book. If you have a quick 50 seconds, we cordially invite you to share your feedback, comments, or any ideas you wish to convey. Your thoughts on what you've garnered from this book are valued and awaited.

Here are the steps to leave your review:

1. Open your mobile camera.
2. Access the link by scanning the QR code below.
3. Follow the link to write your review.

Or visit:

https://condesa07.com/amazonReview/SummerColoringBook

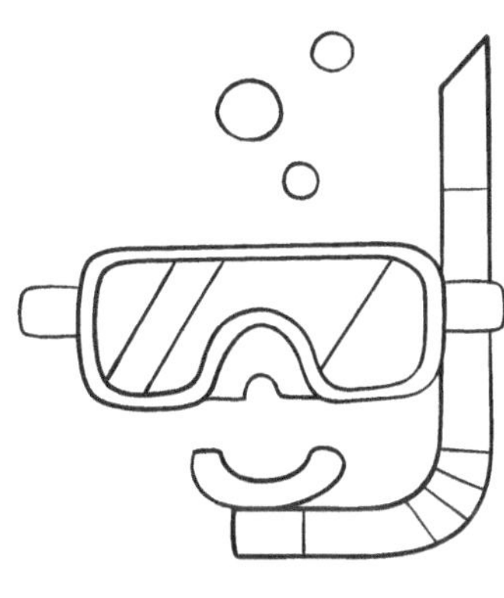